# Those Who Wait

BY JANE SMITH

**DORRANCE**
PUBLISHING CO
EST. 1920
PITTSBURGH, PENNSYLVANIA 15238

Dorrance Publishing Co
585 Alpha Drive
Pittsburgh, PA 15238
Visit our website at *www.dorrancebookstore.com*

ISBN: 978-1-6366-1171-6
EISBN: 978-1-6366-1762-6

# Those Who Wait

# CHAPTER 1

At the outbreak of World War II, my father enlisted in the army and volunteered for the infantry. He told my mother he was going to "kill Hitler." She was left to care for my brother, who was three years old.

He landed on D-Day and was an infantry lieutenant in charge of a platoon. When I was about four years old, I found a few pictures of him sitting with some soldiers and a small, black dog around tents. I was most interested in the little dog and would ask my father, "What was her name, again?" I hoped he would tell me more about her. She was a cute, little black and white dog.

My father would say, "We called her Spritz, because she was a little Spritz dog."

My father never talked about the war, but there was one story he would tell:

> "War is not what you picture if you are not there. One day a soldier came running around the corner of a brick building that had been hit by a grenade. All of a sudden we were face to face. We were both pointing our guns at each other. He was German, I was American. He looked about my age. In a split second, we

each lowered our guns, turned, and walked away. We were not able to kill each other that time."

When I was twelve, he took me to see the movie *Judgement at Nuremberg*. We were always poor growing up, and that was the first movie I had ever seen and would be the only time we would ever go to a movie together. It was really cold the night we went. We had to walk about ten blocks to the theater. I was wearing my best soled shoes and had to put cardboard in them whenever I had to walk far in the snow. It only helped for a short time, but it was a positive motivation to keep going.

For me the movie was frightening. I hardly remember walking home, except that we talked very little. Finally, he said, "I hope you will never forget that movie. People can commit terrible atrocities to one another. We are our brother's keeper. When we see evil, we must be brave and find the truth."

After the war, my second brother, myself, and my younger sister were born, and my father began a business of tuning, restoring, moving, selling, and buying used pianos. We moved ten times by the time I was sixteen years old, mostly because we lived in the rural state of South Dakota and his piano business was labor intensive, including many hours of travel. One of the most memorable places we lived was, for me, a small apartment above Main Street of Rapid City when I was about five years old.

Across the street was the Sioux Indian Museum. It was beautiful. There were relics and clothing from the Sioux behind glass, and there were also scenes behind glass windows depicting the everyday lives of Indians with their original clothing, moccasins, blankets, buffalo tents, and little kids. In the back room were real stuffed animals: bobcats, birds, owls, porcupines, rabbits, wolves, and coyotes. I spent a lot of time at the museum. The women and men who cared for it were very tolerant of me and always acted like they were glad to see me, though I'm sure I must have often been a nuisance like many 6-year-olds.

The museum was built with stones layered one on top of the other, and they stuck out at different levels, making them really great for climbing. I could climb around the whole building without getting down, after a lot of practice. There were many Indians who would gather in the park outside of their museum to sleep and eat, some would drink wine and others just pretty much spent days and nights there.

"The Great Spirit" was often mentioned by regulars at Sioux Park, and I began to think more about who I was. I would ask myself *"who am I,"* over and over again. I would try to sleep at night in the small room I shared with my sister by repeating the question *"who am I,"* over and over again. It seemed I could disappear into a strange world of a totally vast universe and look at myself from outside of myself. It was both really scary and exciting. One day at school, when we were learning to read, I had a strange feeling the elephant on one of the pages was turning white and began to walk. It was very scary, and I told the teacher I was sick and wanted my dad to come and get me. She sent me to the nurse's office, and they called my father. When he came to get me, I was shaky and feeling cold. He drove me home in his Studebaker pick-up (which I loved), and as we rode along, he asked me what happened. I told him about the white elephant, and how it was walking in the book.

He scratched his head and said, "Were you afraid?"

"Yes." I said.

Then he asked, "Is there anything else you are afraid of at school?"

"Not really," I answered.

He told me it is not unusual to be afraid when a person is doing something new.

"Sometimes you will learn very interesting and complicated things in school. "Reading is a very complicated thing and it is fascinating to learn," he explained. "Do you think you could have been surprised that the elephant was kinda coming to life as you were learning about it?"

Still the elephant remained a mystery, and another strange question to wonder about – *"Was it real? Was I even real?"*

He continued, "Do your friends at the Indian Museum talk to you about the Great Spirit?"

Of course he knew they did, because I already told him about that.

"Well," he continued, "I believe in the Great Spirit, also. It is a mystery that no-one understands, for sure, but is in the entire universe and it designs and organizes everything. It is not scary, really. So all your life you will try to figure this out, and I'm just saying it's okay to do that. It's what we all do, and it is okay."

I felt the elephant was likely just my imagination, but that learning was full of truths and untruths; that the "spirit" of life was a great mystery and a constant journey to finding truth.

We were taught about the importance of sharing, and that it is a core value which sometimes results in positive and negative experiences. I shared when it was unnecessary, and even harmful; sometimes sharing things that were not mine to share. One day I gave my father's ties away to the people who sat on the sidewalk below our apartment. They must have wondered why I gave them his ties. I'm sure he wondered.

My mom was small, very attractive, and proud of her attractiveness. She would spend hours at the kitchen table with fingernail polish and hours changing her clothes. We shared a distant and mute relationship. She would always ask me a recurring question, which threatened my self-esteem to its core.

"What kind of get-up are you wearing today?' she would ask nearly every day.

I do not recall many conversations between my mother and me. She was not a very active person. She was a quiet person and her routine was quite solitary. She sat at a table during the day with her fingernail polish and some magazines with Hollywood stories and gossip. She ate very little and was very concerned with staying "thin and fit."

Tuning and repairing pianos throughout western South Dakota, and even into Montana and Nebraska, was not an easy job. Sometimes

I would ride along with my father in his Studebaker pick-up on trips to small towns and rural farms, if he was going to be gone all day, so I could "see the world." He was fun to be with on those trips, but he could become very depressed when we were home in the more mundane activities of everyday life. He was also a very generous person, and when we traveled together, we would pick up hitch-hikers who were always in need of food, clothing, and shelter, often giving them some of the money he made from tuning and fixing pianos. Hitch-hikers were usually people he called "hobos", and there were also many Indians walking along the roads.

He said Indians were mostly walking to relatives' and friend's homes. Indians in our state were Sioux Indians, whose ancestors had been killed by early settlers who were afraid of them and wanted their land. He would talk about how "everybody has a culture" and that culture is precious and a deep life inside all of us. We talked about many different ideas and opinions, one was the word "empathy," was it a talent or was it learned? He liked the poet Carl Sandburg and believed that people make change in the world mostly by talking to each other at their own kitchen tables, and that people generally wanted what was good and fair.

He would say, "No ruler who has ever tried to destroy the people, ultimately, won. Hitler is dead and the fascists were stopped. Proof that people are ultimately good, just living in a bad world, sometimes."

He also talked about Eli Wiesel and his book, *Night*, and would become very emotional, nearly crying. He would say, "Just think about it and think about the movie *Judgement at Nuremberg*. Many of his relatives died by being gassed in the ovens or starved and then thrown into the mass graves there. But he, just a young boy in that deadly concentration camp, lived to tell us all about it."

Some people said my father was "shell-shocked" in World War II; what we say is PTSD today. I don't know, but he seemed to want to disappear into the world of pianos. He would change sad conversations by adding, "Music is a universal language."

We often talked about "the Great Spirit". That conversation began when he would say, "I mean nobody has ever been able to definitely know what God is. No one has ever proved they know the mind of God, if there is a God, or if there is not a God. Organized religion is a dangerous thing because it always presents ideas that cannot be proven."

From there we would move on to all kinds of possibilities, sometimes even the real possibility that we are not the only people in the universe.

There was one particular year, however; when we became a typical fifties family, I think. Tom and I had a large paper route, we got a dog, my mother wore nice dresses and clothes, Nancy found friends next door, and Bob started college. It was 1956, and we got our first television. This new addition to our lives changed my mother more than anyone else in our family. She loved all the soap operas, *The Guiding Light*, *As the World Turns*, and shows like *The Honeymooners* and *I Love Lucy*. She began spending hours watching television, and my father began taking her out to eat and they would go dancing. She was able to buy new clothes, makeup, and accessories.

My father continued spending time on his piano business, refinishing and restoring pianos in the garage and tuning for schools and private homes. As my mother began to find her way, the rest of our family became calmer. My younger sister, Nancy, and I become closer and would stay up late at night talking and listening to the radio. Nancy was the person who seemed most involved in trying to give attention to my mother's eccentricities, but the television became my mother's caregiver.

# CHAPTER 2

By the time I began my 11th grade year in high school, Bob's college was no longer affordable, and Bob became a "beatnik" who argued over almost everything. Tom finished high school and was learning about the piano business. My parents moved again, and Nancy went with them.

I missed Nancy because we had become close and shared many similarities. We both had hair that was more red, like our Irish mother's side, neither of us liked makeup and never wore fingernail polish, and we were both interested in the mysteries of the stars and planets, what we called "the Universe". We believed in horoscopes and sometimes visited fortune tellers together. However, Nancy questioned her sexuality, and wanted me to call her "Chip" privately. She did not want me to tell anyone, and I didn't because people were very judgmental during that time. Growing up as a girl in South Dakota in the fiftiess and sixtiess was extremely confining and uncomfortable. There was little to no support for any girl who strayed from the "norm" of being what is called a "girly-girl" today. Those of us who chose any kind of road less traveled were ostracized and bullied. Nancy was not even close to thinking she could ever disclose her personality as "Chip" to anyone outside of me. Fortunately, my father was always very accepting of other people's choices, teaching us that as long as you are not hurting yourself or someone or something else, it's okay. But Nancy was not ready to trust anyone with her identity. Nancy, like my father, loved music and the pianos, which she taught freely to others. She had quite a few girlfriends who, together, started a softball team.

After Nancy moved out with my parents, I stayed in the old house to finish high school by taking my junior and senior years in one year. I registered my schedule at the school after getting it approved at the office.

Unfortunately by the summer, when I finished my last class as scheduled, my school would not give me my diploma. A new school counselor would not accept my last summer school credits, would not explain why, and eventually said he would send me my diploma after it "cleared." He never sent it. After working really hard and taking an overload of courses, the roadblock seemed too heavy to move.

Girls and women were treated very unfairly during the sixties. The expectations were that girls got married and took care of the house and kids, and men worked. So not having a high school diploma was acceptable for girls, especially if your family was low income. We moved a lot and I came to know many Sioux Indian families. In those times, and even now, they were not treated as potential high school or college graduates, either. Those of us who were not part of the "norm" were considered to be less.

My first job was working the early morning shift as kitchen help in a nursing home, my second was as a housekeeper, and my third was working as a nurse's aide, all in the same nursing home. The hardest job was my last job at that nursing home, when I began working as a nurses' aide. I had always wanted to be a nurse, but that first job was a horrible experience, because I was not prepared to see the difficulties of old age. Many people had bedsores and were unable to walk, see, hear, or even eat. I wanted to believe the elderly would talk to me, offer me candy, and tell me stories of the past but, instead there seemed to be only suffering, sadness, and death. It was alarming to discover that life is not always what it appears . I quit and became a waitress.

Waitressing was hard. Guys would want waitresses to treat them as special people, flirting and make embarrassing talk. Some guys were okay, but many were bullies and rude. After work my time was spent at the library and walking around the different neighborhoods in town, searching for someone who might listen to my stories of failures.

During my walks one day, I decided to visit an elderly woman who often waved to me while she sat on the front porch of her rooming house. It was an old, run down house near the library. I began to talk to her on the porch. Her name was Lillian.

She told me she was in her 90's and had no children or family. After visiting her for many weeks, she invited me to knock on her door if she was not outside and visit her inside. She said her room was 306. One day when I knocked on the door, a man about 70 years old answered the door. He had thick, unruly white hair, smiley eyes, and was about 5'2". He wore large black trousers and a large white shirt tucked in with a belt. I asked him if Lillian was there. He took a small notebook and pen out of the pocket on the front of his shirt, where the pen had left many blue ink marks.

> He wrote, *"I am Homer Kent, deaf mute."*
> I wrote back, *"I am Jane, and am looking for Lillian."*
> He wrote, *"She is old lady in hall room 306. This is 304."*

Days later I saw Homer again on the street by the library, and I realized that I had often seen him in the past but never really paid attention to him. I waved to him and walked toward him. He remembered me, and we began writing notes back and forth in his notebook. We began a long friendship. He was well-known by the shopkeepers in town because he worked as a dishwasher, dry cleaning help, and odd janitorial jobs.

Homer and I would sit on benches at Sioux Park, visit the creeks and feed ducks, and have coffee in the cafes around town where he worked as a dishwasher. He would write many notes about his long and storied past and about his life as a shoemaker and cobbler. He had a large wooden kit filled with all the tools and metal molds of feet a person used to make and fix shoes. When I tried to understand Homer, I would imagine what his past must have been like. He was born around 1890, even before cars were part of everyday lives. He was in his twenties during WW1 and in his forties s during WW2. I tried to imagine his past life, and what it must have been like to be deaf, remembering how my father always talked about how "everybody has a deep culture" inside.

Homer also taught me a lot of signs from the American Sign Language (ASL), and he gave me cards with the sign-language manual alphabet. He worked at a drycleaners in town that was owned by a man who had a deaf son who attended school in Sioux Falls at the School for the Deaf. I met many of his younger friends who came home from school every summer and on holidays. They were a great motivation for me, because they were a tightly knit group who were willing to give me time and attention. They helped me create more serious goals toward work and my future and encouraged me to try for a job at the School for the Deaf in Sioux Falls.

That fall I took a Greyhound Bus to Sioux Falls, hoping for a job at that school. Unfortunately, my interview did not go well because I did not have a high school diploma. I returned home and began trying to help Homer get medical attention because he was often using the sign "blood" and "sick." We visited a doctor and, eventually, he was diagnosed with cancer. I began going to appointments and to the hospital to interpret for him. One day Homer wanted me to ask the church minister across the street if he would be able to mail Homer a copy of his sermon every week.

When I asked the minister if Homer could get a copy of his sermons, he said, "For you to be visiting him at that house is extremely careless and unsafe, and if "Gomer" wants a copy of the sermon, he needs to make that request in person."

I was angry with the minister. After a few days, I asked my dad for help.

"What should I do about this minister?" I asked.

My father stood attentively and said sternly, "Tell the minister that a survivor of the Holocaust, Eli Wiesel, wrote a book, 'Night" about the Holocaust, and said, 'the first word in responsibility is response.' He also said 'the opposite of love is not hate, it is indifference'. In fact, just write him a letter, no need to approach him in person."

My letter to the minister went like this:

> *Dear Pastor Dave, am writing you to again ask if you would send a copy of your sermons to my friend Homer K, who lives in the house across the street from your church. As I said when we last spoke, Homer is deaf and is interested in what your church is about.*
>
> *My father was a soldier in the infantry during World War 2, and I told him I asked you about sending Homer a copy of your sermons and that you said Homer had to ask you, instead of me, because I should not be visiting Homer. He said that Eli Wiesel, who was a victim in the concentration camps of Hitler's Nazi Germany, who survived and wrote about his experiences in his book, 'Night. He quoted the book for you; "the first word in responsibility is response" and also, 'the opposite of love is not hate, it is indifference'. I hope you will be able to send Homer copies of your sermons, his address is 401, St. Joe Street, apt 304. Thanks, Jane N."*

Nothing changed for about two weeks. Then, one day, Homer showed me a copy of Pastor Dave's sermon that he got in his mail. It seemed hard to believe that something so simple could be so difficult.

Through my friendship with Homer, I got a job at the hospital on the graveyard shift and began working on the cancer ward as a nurses' aide.

Working in the hospital on the night shift was a tough experience. Most of the patients on the 4th floor were terminally ill cancer patients. Few ever left the floor unless they died. I guess the "bright spot" was the wing on the 4th floor where there was a Coronary Care unit. There were about ten rooms with patients who did not have cancer. They were patients recovering from heart attacks, and some younger patients who had been in serious accidents which left them totally or partially paralyzed. There was a lot to learn on the fourth floor. One nurse explained to me, "When you care for people, try to treat them as your own brother or sister, or as angels in disguise who are watching your every move. The Golden Rule."

Many nurses on my floor had served in WWII. They were detail oriented and strict. Beds had to be made with no wrinkles, all patients were on strict schedules, and charts had to be perfect.

Before each shift, we would have floor meetings. The nurses went through their daily log of patients and gave us real time updates on the condition of each patient and their daily activities. We were assigned to patients and wrote down every detail of their care. Notes like: "*John T. : Ambulate 4x daily. Elevate L. leg when in bed. Force fluids. Vitals Q 4 hours. Intake and Output. Monitor IV's*" would outline our tasks. We were usually assigned four to six patients. As I moved on in the health care system through the next forty-five years, I often wished floor meetings would be mandatory, instead of being eliminated as time changed the face of care.

While nurses taught us the "fundamentals" of care, they did not teach us how to cope with death and suffering. We were not taught the stages of grief. In fact we were encouraged to be "tough" and not wear our heart on our sleeve. They said we should follow the Golden Rule but taught us how to not get close to patients or families. It was a contradiction which was difficult to accept.

Sometimes we would all go out for coffee after work and talk about our shift. During these informal meetings, older aides often gave advice on how to deal with the suffering and death on the fourth floor. Sometimes we would sit for hours talking about the cancer floor. Conversations were generally not so much about individual physical care, but how we should carry out emotional care for patients. One day I began talking about our breakroom being only feet away from many private rooms with terminally ill patients.

"Don't you guys think we should not smoke in the break-room, because smoke goes into patients' rooms and all the way through the halls?" I asked. I was not a smoker at the time, and I knew this might upset the aides who smoked.

Theresa, an older aide, kind of laughed and said, "Well, they are already dying. I mean, what harm is it going to do?"

I answered, "Ok, I know, but when I answer Helen's call light, she says 'Oh those cigarettes smell so good, could you give me a straw so I could just pretend?' I mean she is dying from lung cancer. Do I get a straw and give it to her, or do we just quit smoking next to her room?"

Debbie said, "I say just give her a straw because there is no rule saying we cannot smoke in the breakroom, everybody does it, including the nurses."

"Sure," I answered. "And if the nurses see her with a straw, we will get in trouble, and is that helpful to her in any way?"

Theresa agreed. "You know," she said, "this is a dilemma we deal with every day. I mean if, for example, Mr. Smith wants to get up, but his care plan does not allow it, do we side with him or the professionals? We know him better on a day-to-day basis than they do."

Debbie interrupted and said, "Remember when Mr. Gray wanted to get up that one night? I mean, he had brain cancer, had seizures every hour or less, and we all thought he was not even conscious anymore. And remember the night we checked on him and right out of nowhere he wakes up and says, 'Will you help me get up so I can look out the window?' Remember? And we got scared because we thought he was not even able to talk anymore?"

Then, looking at all of us, she continued, "So we got him up. We helped him go to the window. He looks out and says, 'Now I want to lay back down, I am ready to die.' So we laid him down and we went and told Withers, the charge nurse, and she got mad at us and thought we were trying to joke with her. We told her to go see him. By then, he had died. She never believed us and was upset with us and told us what we were doing was a very bad joke. It was not a joke."

We often discussed ways to improve the work of nurses' aides. The first step, we decided, would start with taking down the wall between nurses' aides and the doctors and nurses. We needed to be considered as professionals and workers with a defined role in caregiving techniques. We needed to have training and be licensed as direct caregivers. We needed to be seen as professionals. As my life as an aide progressed, I would remember the importance of this idea; that we should be considered as equals and as professionals in our own right.

# CHAPTER 3

Working at the hospital was really starting to get me down. Homer was failing, and I feared he would be admitted to the cancer floor and die there. I helped him move to two different apartments, hoping he would be more comfortable. He was past seventy years old now. Daily life was becoming difficult for him, but he asked me to keep checking in with him and not let him go to the hospital. He wanted to stay in his home. I would buy groceries and make meals for him that would be easy to eat, take his laundry to the laundromat, and spend time learning more signs. We signed almost everything, but I was slow. Homer seemed to enjoy teaching me signs; some were really beautiful, others humorous.

There were very few visits from other people, and it was painful for me to think of Homer being home, waiting for me to check up on him. When people are housebound with age related issues or are not able to go out independently, they seem suspended in time. They are always waiting for someone, and often the one who they are hoping to see does not show up. Homer was my good friend, and I did not want to disappoint him by not showing up or by being late. I did not want to cause him the emotional pain of waiting.

It was legal to drink at the age of eighteen in South Dakota in bars that sold 3.2 beer. Nancy and her friends would meet at the bowling alley to drink at night, and I started to spend time meeting up with them and drinking. My family had a history of drinking too much, but I felt being with Nancy helped me get over the stress of working in the hospital. Along with drinking, I started smoking a lot and wasting a lot of my paycheck on the lifestyle that involved bars and socializing – spending money playing pool, buying drinks and food, and giving money out to others, including food and needs for Homer. Once there were checks called "counterchecks." They were available in bars and grocery stores everywhere. These counterchecks only needed the name of the person you were writing the check to and your signature and address on the bottom. I started writing checks to almost anyone. When they could not be covered at the bank because I had no account, I would get a notice in the mail to pay the bank for that check within 10-15 days.

Mostly, I ignored the notices thinking, *why does the bank care if they don't get all the money? Nothing will probably ever happen to me.*

But it did.

One day, when I was at a bar, the county sheriff arrested me for my bad checks and I had to stay in jail overnight. The next day, the judge told me if I ever wrote another bad check, he would send me to the women's pen. I paid the checks off, but after they were all paid, I started writing them again. This time the police went to my father's piano tuning shop and told him they were going to arrest me for bad checks, again. He did not have the money to pay them and came to my apartment to tell me I should probably leave town, get a job, and send money back to the courts. I had to move away; he was right.

It was especially difficult for me to leave because I knew Homer would be alone. My father said he would take over visits and watch out for Homer.

I called a friend of my brothers who was working in the library of a University in New York binding books, and I asked him if I could visit. He said it would be okay. A friend lent me some money, and I took a Greyhound bus to Rochester, New York. Within a few months, he and I moved to Buffalo and began "organizing" for the revolution. We were in a socialist group and were the contacts for Buffalo. We found an apartment in a slum on Chippewa Street next to Dewey's Diner.

The apartment manager was a Polish immigrant. When he rented it to us, he said, "It's sixty-dollars a month. If you can pay, that's good. If you can't, that's okay, too."

Shortly after we rented the apartment on Chippewa Street, I called my father to let him know I would try to start paying my bad checks. He told me Homer had died. That was hard for me, because no one in my life, at that time, knew Homer, and all the time we spent together was really hard to talk about with others. But at least he did not have to go to the cancer floor and die alone.

Chippewa Street, in the late sixties and seventies, was very poor. We were able to rent a run-down third story apartment next to Dewey's Diner. The diner was a place where men bet on horse racing and had gambling tables. Expensive cars were parked outside, day and night. There were gunfights and wars fought at Dewey's. Our apartment building was part of the property and management of Dewey's.

I got a job at Buffalo Columbus Hospital just a few blocks away. The nurse said, "I never met anyone from South Dakota, and I never hired anyone from Chippewa St."

My job was to clean the OR after surgeries and transport patients from the ER to surgery.

Don drove his VW back and forth to Rochester and New York, organizing for the revolution. I contributed by paying our rent and providing some food. We mostly ate rice and canned peas mixed together. Don did not spend much time at the apartment, and I worked overtime as much as possible at Buffalo Columbus. After work I always went home because we were very poor and there was no money to spend on anything but food and rent.

One day when Don came back, he said we should move to Chicago, where his group needed people to organize and leaflet. I had worked for over six months at the hospital and was learning a lot at work, but I decided to go with him. I really did not know Don very well or even cared about his politics much, but I did not want to be alone at the apartment. Don had been wanting to leave for some time, and his friends in the "movement" were not interested in Buffalo and Chippewa Street. Don wanted to leave that day. He had some books and clothes, and I had only a few clothes and work uniforms. We went to a payphone where he called someone in his group, and later that day we left for Chicago.

# CHAPTER 4

After we moved to Chicago, I began looking for work and got lost on the El-Train. When I got off, I saw a large brick building with a black wrought iron fence and a sign that read:

*Belden Manor Shelter Home*

I went in to apply for work.

A woman at the front desk gave me an application, and she asked me to sit down and wait for an interview. Soon, she brought me to Mr. Caldwell's office. It was a very large office. There were heads of animals mounted on his walls – a tiger, a zebra, some birds, gazelles, crocodiles, and other types of wild animals. Mr. Caldwell appeared to be a safari hunter.

Mr. Caldwell was a large and very well dressed-man about 45-years old. He read my application and asked: "What shift do you want?"

I said, "I don't care."

He replied, "I would say you could work graveyard, but there are no white people on graveyard. So I have nothing for you today."

"I don't care if there are no white people working that shift, it's okay with me. I don't care," I said.

He stared at me and said, "You might not care, but they do. You will be isolated."

I just needed a job. I asked, "Could I have a chance, even for one night?"

"Sure," he said. Then added, "Tonight, be here by 9:30 to check in. Wear a uniform. Front desk will tell you how to enter the building."

After I stopped at the front desk to confirm my new job, the secretary walked me through a back hallway to an outside elevator. She gave me an index card with instructions for that night.

Walking away I could hardly believe I actually got a job in Carl Sandburg's Chicago; home of my favorite writer and "The People Yes." However, I also worried Mr. Caldwell did not explain, or even seem to care about, what was expected of me while working with residents at Belden Manor. It took me a few hours to get back to the apartment because I was lost, but many people directed me home safely and quite easily. That night I found my way back to work riding the EL-Train.

The elevator was old and shaky. The pulley that carried it up and down was easily seen through a space between the floor and the door. It stopped awkwardly, a little before my third floor destination, then jerked and stopped again until the door slid open with a loud clang, and I walked directly into line with a fast moving crowd of walkers and smokers. In the crowd was a woman pushing piles of cigarette butts and tobacco with a large red dust mop. She told me to follow her, and we walked to a small office-like room in the hallway. There was no door to the room.

She said, "I am the charge aide here on swing shift, and I will show you what we do. First, you will be alone here, there is only one aide on this wing during graveyard. A nurse will visit two times every night, around midnight to give you a report, and around 4 A.M. to hear your report. There are twenty-two people, right now, on this wing. Down the hall to your left is a hall that leads to the other wings.

There is no need for you to go there, unless the nurse in charge tells you to go there."

"This wing is open, and patients can come and go as they choose throughout the night. Many sleep in different rooms and with different people. We cannot stop them, so just don't go into any rooms. Your job is to clean up the cigarettes in this hall, stay in this office, and talk to patients when they visit. Many people here are from Cook County homeless missions, some are from the insane asylums, and some are from jails. Some people have been here for a long time, others just came. They will come into the office starting at 5 A.M. to get meds and cigs. Instructions for meds are in the med-box. I will show you how to access that and how to dispense meds."

"There is a paper next to the Bugler tobacco pouches where you mark a X with 'Five Cents' next to each patient who gets tobacco. The state reimburses, so make sure you check the box. Just take a break here in the office, you will have time. Did you bring a sandwich? The break room is not very close to you, and it is best to stay out because there is no one who can cover you if you leave. That's about it. The nurse comes at midnight. I'm on my way home, now."

That night pretty much played out exactly like she told me it would. I spent my time sweeping up cigarettes, talking to the people who sat or walked in the halls, not going in the rooms, and ignoring the flow of people who randomly seemed to go into and out of rooms. The nurse came on the noisy elevator at midnight and 4 A.M. I could hear the elevator when she was on her way up and going down. In the morning, people would line up for meds. The first week was difficult, because not everyone wanted a pouch of Bugler, so I could not ask their name. The people who did not want Bugler were reluctant to identify themselves. That was a problem; however, the next night the charge nurse helped me by giving me profiles for different residents so I could remember who was who. There were only about seven or eight people who did not smoke.

Night shift was pretty easy, in some ways. Unlike the hospitals and nursing homes, people who lived at Beldon Manor were generally oriented to self-only. There was a visible and invisible boundary line – a kind of warm or cool vibe which hung over us when we interacted. People who lived at Beldon Manor seemed to follow self-made patterns for their daily lives. What may appear to be random activity in the halls, and throughout the day and night, were mostly individual routines. Much the same as people create in the "outside world."

Growing up I knew some members of my family were believed to have mental health issues. We hardly talked about it, and when I met people living at Beldon, I expected there would be people like others I knew . There was an uncle on my father's side who heard voices and was always very depressed and disoriented. There was my own mother, who sometimes spent hours doing nothing but sitting on the porch, or inside, and stare off to some distant place. Even my own sister, Nancy, who would switch between being Nancy to a guy named Chip, changing her voice when each person presented. I did not see her sexuality as a personality issue, but I did wonder why she talked in different voices. I knew she heard voices, and I often wondered if it was something inherited in our family. These were some of the personalities I expected to see at Belden.

I felt working at Belden would be a good chance for me to try to become more familiar with some of the issues facing people who live with mental health issues. My rounds consisted of sweeping the cigarettes up in the halls and seeing as much as possible without crossing privacy lines. Some people would stand in the doorways of rooms, guarding entrances, others would play radios too loud and had to be reminded to turn down the volume. One resident would play "The Lion Sleeps Tonight" over and over on his recorder. He would stand in his room, looking out, rarely sleeping. Others were in constant motion – walking in and out of rooms, opening and closing doors. The longer I worked at Belden, the more I appreciated the value of sweeping the halls, because it allowed me to enter the flow of life there.

Some people did not smoke and did not pace the halls. One woman wrote in tablets, constantly.

Another woman would come to the "office" and want to talk. Looking back I feel bad I was not good at listening to her.

I tried to give her compliments and advice saying, "you are really a very interesting person, could you possibly get out of here and get your own place?"

That was my standard response to her, because she would talk about how much she hated being "trapped" in Belden.

One night she was waiting in the office and was standing behind the chair, where no-one was supposed to be at that time. When I came into the small room, she picked up the chair and threatened to kill me.

"I am going to beat you to death because you are a Nazi, Stassi. I know who you are and I am going to kill you," she yelled.

I did not respond. I was surprised and afraid of her.

She continued, "I knew you were a spy! I remember you from when you gave me shock treatment after the war. I know you are a Nazi!"

She smashed the chair on the desk and walked toward me with the broken chair. Then she threw the chair on the floor, pushed me aside, and walked out. I was very afraid of her and rang for help. The night nurse and an aide came to my hall within 15 minutes, which seemed like hours.

When they arrived, they checked her room and said, "She is sleeping. She does this sometimes. She'll be okay."

I asked if she ever hurt anyone.

The nurse said, "Not yet, and she has been here for years, but maybe just don't talk to her a lot. Sometimes people do not think there is anything wrong with them. She is one of those people. No matter what she does or you do, she does not believe there is anything wrong with her. There is something wrong with her physical brain and that could be very dangerous. That is who Hitler, himself, was. It is not about how much you care about them, it is about them believing that there is absolutely nothing wrong with them."

As time went on, I began to better understand the deep and mysterious mental health issues some people struggled with in their daily lives. While many seemed to have extreme memories from past traumatic experiences, others seemed to have issues which sprung from damages to their physical brain. I also noticed many residents experienced mood-swings at the same time every night. Some people started talking to themselves, pacing the floor, and changing their personalities around the same time every night.

*This is true also of my sister.* I would think to myself.

The saddest and most frustrating part for me, while working with people at Belden, was how they were branded with the stereotype of "crazy." They were all lumped into the same category, and treatment was generic. While people with physical disabilities might get physical therapy, people with mental disabilities were given cigarettes and hallways. The brain was, and still is, seen as a moral object we can control and direct to be good or bad, while the body gets many "do-overs" when it isn't acting normally.

Also, it became more obvious how mental health issues create extremely difficult times for everyone involved in day-to-day activities. Residents would ask if anyone had called or planned to visit them. It was heartbreaking to realize they, like everyone in this world – from young children to the very old – were waiting for someone and were missing someone.

Sadly residents at Belden seemed very alone, and I wondered what happened to their past families and friends. I studied some of their charts so I might better understand how they ended up in Belden, smoking, pacing the halls, and talking to themselves.

Many past histories were almost blank, and some were simply diagnosed as "institutionalized." Whatever happened to them which resulted in being institutionalized was not charted. Some people who were diagnosed as "institutionalized" were mostly older men. Oddly none of them smoked, and they were quiet and withdrawn. They did not appear at night, when other residents were smoking, walking the halls, and opening and closing doors.

Younger residents had more extensive histories. Some were abandoned as children and grew up in abusive foster or relative's homes, others were criminally charged with public nuisance crimes and unsubstantiated sex crimes, and some were victims of sex crimes and incest. Others had endured shock treatments or had been incarcerated for non-violent crimes, were traumatized, and acted out when released back into their communities.

I felt bad for people who lived at Belden, and I wished there were better places for all of them other than jails, which were much worse. It seemed society was unable to create humane settings for them, or places where they could be properly diagnosed and helped. I also felt a little better knowing at least at Belden, they were saved from being homeless and alone on the streets of Chicago. Many residents had no visitors. Charts had very little information about friends or relatives. Most people at Belden were alone, seemingly having no connections with their past lives. No hugs, no laughter, and no communication with friends or family members.

Another discouraging and surprising fact about Belden Manor was the entire place, which housed about 100 residents, had only one doctor. How could one doctor have time to do anything for them besides write their prescriptions?

Night shift had one charge nurse, one night watchman, and the rest of us were nurses' aides. The charge nurse patiently taught what could be called "Mental Health Work 101." Her name was Ora. She was around 60 years old, a fairly tall and thin black woman. Ora explained how she thought nurses' aides' work should be considered a profession. She believed a good aide had a combination of knowledge and empathy. Ora did not talk to me very much, but she did share some of her life story and how she became a nurse. She always encouraged me to work at being a good nurse's aide.

Ora said, "If you are good at being an aide, you will always have a job. Actually there is a greater demand for aides than for nurses because a good aide can understand the language of one-on-one care and that is the most important job in care facilities. As caregivers we need to develop a deep understanding of others, so we can understand everything possible about the people we care about and care for. It is a real profession, just a hidden one."

"Did you ever hear the quote from Michelangelo about the marble statues he carved?" she asked.

"He said, 'I saw the angel in the marble and I chiseled till I set it free.' That should be our goal as caregivers. We need to find the person in the patient, listen to what they say, and work to set them free."

I will always be grateful to Ora for talking to me and checking on me at midnight and at 4 A.M. Ora encouraged me to be grateful. I have a passion for caregiving and to work hard to develop good communication and connections with others.

Ora suggested I take lunch breaks in the break room, and she offered to have someone take over my hall. I was really glad to be able to leave my hall for a while. Mr. Caldwell's warning about the breakroom was wrong.. The aides were black and Filipino, and there were no white people so that was true. However, I was not isolated. People were nice. I was actually embarrassed to have stayed away from the break room, but I did not want to talk about what Mr. Caldwell had said.

As time went on, I was included in plans to start a union at Belden Manor. Aides told me to keep it between us, but one morning Mr. Caldwell arrived before 6 A.M. and questioned me about rumors of a union. I told him I had heard rumors but nothing more. He perked up and wanted to know more. I answered that no-one really knew much else. That night, on break, I told other aides about his visit. They became very concerned and uneasy.

An aide cautioned me saying, "Never, under any circumstances, talk to Mr. Caldwell about anything regarding any rumors or about anything."

She continued, "You are the only white person here. He will try to use you to his advantage. That is what will happen, believe me".

The next morning, Mr. Caldwell arrived early wanting to talk, but I avoided him. I felt, perhaps, he was one of those people who did not think there was anything wrong with him.

Residents and the help at Belden Manor taught me to be true to myself and to keep going no matter how difficult things might get. Their personal stories have been seldom told in Hollywood or written in schoolbooks. There were times when it seemed none of the residents at Belden Manor cared about me, about themselves, or about anything except pacing up and down the hall, smoking, or staring into space. It was frustrating, because I wanted to believe there was nothing wrong with them to be "fixed." Maybe they just did not want to be nice. They seemed to never think about anyone but themselves. Aides in the breakroom helped me understand mental illness as a silent disease that is often better understood if we learn to accept their silence and become more quiet ourselves. We do not talk loud or argue with them and, most importantly, do not judge them.

Working at Belden was not easy, because there seemed to be no solutions for the insidious disease of mental illness. Many residents were physically very healthy and even more physically attractive than average people. However, they were caught in mental traps. To this very day, I do not think there are many people who understand mental illness and fewer who have found solutions.

One person who has contributed the best solutions and information about mental illness is E. Fuller Torrey. He is a leading psychiatrist and Schizophrenia researcher who has written 20 books on mental illness. His most recent book is *Insane Consequences: How the Mental Health Industry Fails the Mentally Ill*. He grew up with a sister who was schizophrenic and, in 1998, he founded the Treatment Advocacy Center, which maintains a concentrated effort to reform laws and improve the lives of those who are affected by major mental health issues.

In September of 2013, Salon Magazine printed an excerpt from E. Fuller Torrey's book, *American Psychosis*, which explains how mental health issues and care facilities have evolved since the late fifties to the present.

He wrote: "Beginning in the late 1950's, California became the national leader in aggressively moving patients from state hospitals to nursing homes and board-and-care homes, known in other states by names such as group homes, boarding homes, adult care hombres, assisted living facilities, community residential facilities, adult foster homes, transitional living facilities, and residential care facilities. Hospital wards closed as the patients left. By the time Reagan assumed the governorship in 1967, California had already deinstitutionalized more than half of the state hospital patients. That same year, California passed the landmark Lanterman-Petris-Short (LPS) Act, which virtually abolished involuntary hospitalization, except in extreme cases. Thus, by the early 1970's, California had moved most mentally ill patients out of its state hospitals and, by passing LPS, had made it very difficult to get them back into a hospital if they relapsed and needed additional care. California thus became a canary in the coal mine of deinstitutionalization." [1]

He continued, "By 1975, board and care homes had become big business in California. Many of these homes were owned by non-profit chains, such as Beverly Enterprises" (Torrey 2013).[2]

Excerpt from same article: "[In the] 1980's, the problems become national. Until the 1980s, most people in the U.S. were unaware the deinstitutionalization of patients from state mental hospitals was going terribly wrong."[3]

Continuing on after including concerns about incarceration of the mentally ill, he then quotes,

"Sociologist Andrew Scull, in 1981, summaized the economics of the board-and-care industry: 'The logic of the market place suffices to insure that the operators have every incentive to warehouse their

---

[1]  E. Fuller Torrey, "Ronald Reagan's Shameful Legacy: Violence, The Homeless, Mental Illness," *Salon*, September 29, 2013.

[2]  Ibid.

[3]  Ibid.

charges as cheaply as possible, since the volume is inversely proportional to the amount expended on the inmates.'"[4]

Finally, in paragraph ten, he writes: "By the end of the 1980's, the origins of the increasing number of mentally ill homeless persons had become abundantly clear. A study of 187 patients, discharged from Metropolitan State Hospital in Massachusetts, reported 27% had become homeless. In a study of 132 patients, discharged from Columbus State Hospital in Ohio, 36% had become homeless. In 1989, when a San Francisco television station wished to advertise its series on homelessness, it put up posters around the city saying, "You are now walking through America's newest mental institution." Psychiatrist Richard Lamb added: 'Probably nothing more graphically illustrates the problems of deinstitutionalization than the shameful and incredible phenomenon of homeless mentally ill.'"[5]

Belden Manor was a good description of "America's newest mental institution" because it was temporary and without organized care. Residents could walk away from Belden, never to be seen again. They were left alone and without a support system. The main thing which kept residents at Belden was not mental health care but Bugler Tobacco pouches and debilitating medications. Sadly, today, Belden Manor would be considered a good place, because the present-day alternatives in America are jails or homelessness. In my own experience, I have known many people since 2001 who had major mental health issues and became incarcerated or homeless. One person I know was incarcerated over forty-four times in a ten year period and served months in solitary confinement in county jails.

---

[4]  Ibid.
[5]  Ibid.

# CHAPTER 5

Don decided he wanted to move back to South Dakota and run for office as an Independent candidate for the US Senate. Our apartment was in a place which was not very safe and was also a pretty long way to Belden Manor at night. We left Chicago and moved back to South Dakota to Don's parent's house in a small town.

Don's father built roads, and his mother worked in the town's cafe. Don's grandparents were Scandinavians who originally had farms; however, during the depression, they lost their farms and became town people, like many others at the time.

The town had a post office, a pump gas station with a few grocery items inside, a bar, a cafe, a small Lutheran Church, and a small Catholic Church.

He had three sisters, one brother, and his father, who was a road builder with two large Caterpillar vehicles he kept in a barn a few blocks away from their house.

He had a business card that read: "*Ray Hall: Earth Mover*".

Don's mother stayed home raising her kids as they grew up.

She would sometimes say, "When the kids were little, I never went any farther than the clothes-line."

Her name was Annie. She was raised on a farm in the area, but her father died when she was only ten. Her mother sold the farm, and they moved into a larger town. It had a population of about twelve hundred people.

Annie was the oldest, so she stayed home and raised her brother and sisters while her mother worked in the town's small mattress factory. When Annie and Ray were married, she was twenty-one and he was thirty years old. Annie always laughed with this story about her and Ray.

"We met at a small church picnic they had one fall. Ray was there, and we were the last two left anywhere around who hadn't gotten married yet."

Don's idea to run for the Senate as an Independent took all the time and money we had that spring and summer. We lived with Annie and Ray, as well as in abandoned houses in different counties. We painted barns throughout the area. We needed over six-thousand signatures to get on the ballot in South Dakota as an Independent. Our days were mixed with barn painting, gathering signatures, and drinking in small town bars after dark. We showered in the homes of supporters and friends, and ate very little, mostly apples and noon meals in small town cafes around the areas we painted. Those noon meals were a place where Don could talk "politics" to the famers and town laborers.

By the fall deadline, we had more than enough signatures to get on the ballot. Our petitions were dotted with barn paint, some were a little worn, but they were all signed and completed correctly, or so we thought. The night before we drove to the state capitol, we signed our petitions on the back, where there was a place for signing. Unknowingly, we had gotten some of our petitions mixed up. Many days we each had clipboards with the petitions we were circulating; however, we sometimes used each other's clipboard. We did not realize the mistake, because Don and I were the only ones circulating petitions and everything we did, in those days, was as a team. The Senate race was in 1974. It was to be a close race between McGovern (Democrat) and Leo Thorsness (Vietnam war hero and Republican.)

The weekend after we turned our petitions into the Secretary of State, who was a Democrat, we were approached by the Department of Criminal Investigation of South Dakota. We were staying in a small room, which we registered as our residence. It was Sunday morning and there was a knock on the door. I opened the door and two state highway patrol officers were at the door.

They asked, "Are you Jane S.?"

I said, "Yes."

Don came to the door, too. They continued, "We are from the DCI and investigating your petitions. There appears to be a problem, possibly involving fraud and perjury against Jane for falsely circulating petitions. You may need to contact an attorney."

When they left, I was really worried and confused. I had spent many hours and many difficult days helping Don get the signatures he needed and could not understand what was happening.

The following week, the office of the Secretary of State and the Attorney General announced our petitions had been denied due to major discrepancies in the signing of our petitions. The attorney general stated to the press our petitions had been investigated and were denied due to illegal help from socialist organizers from outside the state. Don was characterized as a communist, who had ties with people who worked to get the signatures. Two attorneys helped us and reviewed our case for free. They found the claim by the State was the result of the investigation, which asked different signers of our petitions whether they were asked by a man or a woman. The results of the investigation stated many people said a woman or man asked, while the signatures at the bottom of the petition showed otherwise. So many petitions were denied as was Don's place as an Independent on the ballot. We tried to argue our case in court, but due to time, and the complicated issue, we lost.

Don's failure to appear on the ballot was a huge loss for him. By gathering many signatures and visiting every county in South Dakota, he had gained a lot of support. He bought TV ads and was a regular in newspaper articles. He would have been the first Independent candidate to run for the U.S. Senate in South Dakota in over one hundred years.

After the campaign ended, our relationship of teamwork became weaker. We needed money and jobs. Fall weather was turning colder, and barn painting was over for the year. We decided to move to Sioux City, where the huge meat packing plants were always hiring and, for the next two years, we worked on the line cutting beef. Don boned out chucks and I boned out arms and shanks.

I liked my job, because, for the first time in my life, I was making money. The plant employed over 3,000 workers. Working in the plant was extremely dangerous. Lines would have overloads, and huge portions of meat would stack up near saws and sometimes fall to the floor. Floors were slippery and knives were often worn and dull. Workers were treated badly. Many were hurt, some killed, at the plant. Workers from Mexico, who were trying to immigrate to America, were harassed and intimidated and sometimes arrested while working on the line and taken to Texas, only to be returned a few weeks later. It was a company policy, the purpose of which was to intimidate and threaten them with deportation, much like today. I became a union shop steward and Don organized a new political race for Mayor of Sioux City, along with a new attempt to run for the U.S. House in South Dakota. He was able to get on the ballot in 1976, but only got around two-thousand votes.

Almost all the money we made at our jobs was gone after those campaigns. Our relationship had been stronger as friends than as a couple, and now we were becoming more distant. In hindsight we had a strange relationship. For years I helped finance his ideas and political activities, and I depended on him for companionship.

The Nordic culture is quite unemotional, in the traditional sense of the word. Scandinavians are extremely individualistic and have a difficult time expressing emotions. They separate themselves from one another. Norwegians are historically male dominated. Many last names taken as they immigrated from Norway ended with "son," after the name of the father of the family – Nelson , Anderson, etc. Swedish last names often ended in "datter," which identifies members as daughters of the mother or father, like Helgadatter or Christiansdatter. My paternal grandmother had a Swedish mother and a Danish father. They became involved with the Mormon Church, and her father became a polygamist. When my grandmother was very young, her mother gave her to a cousin in South Dakota so as to remove her from a life in the Mormon Church. While the Nordic Culture may appear to be liberal and focused on humane goals, I believe it is also extremely male dominated and sexist.

Don and I were good friends, but we often argued and disagreed about money and goals. He wanted to use his intelligence to change the world I wanted to use my energy to be part of the world. I always wanted to have children, a lot of children.

We decided to move back to the Black Hills where we could work in the woods, thinning trees with my brother, Bob, who was also an old friend of Don's from their college days.

We began thinning trees by getting bids from the Forest Service. The first summer, we lived in a homemade tent on one of our units. The work was hard, and it wasn't profitable. Saws broke down and cost time and money to fix. Winter weather slowed work down and getting paid took weeks after the jobs were completed. But most importantly, I had our first child – a little girl.

I always wanted to have a large family, but Don and I had no kids for the first seven years we were together. Now I was excited to be having a baby, finally. I went into labor on a cold January day; it was about 20 degrees below zero and we were working in the woods cutting trees. Don took me to the hospital, and within a few hours, the doctor delivered her. I named her Annie. We would have four more kids, all about 20 months apart, and all delivered by the same doctor, who delivered all births naturally – "pregnancy is not a sickness," he would say. Few people were his patients.

We were really broke after Annie was born, borrowing money from anyone we could find, getting food stamps, and arguing. We lived in a rundown, motel-like room for about six months after Annie was born. When Annie was about three months old, I began work as a nurses' aide at the State Hospital for the Severely and Profoundly Retarded. Don stayed home with Anne while I was at work. Soon we were able to move to a more comfortable, upstairs apartment, and I rode to work with other people who worked at the state hospital.

# CHAPTER 6

The State Hospital for the Severely and Profoundly Retarded consisted of a main building, a large workshop where wheel-chairs were created and fixed, a boiler building where a fur-nace burned trash, and eight houses where employees lived. The main building was a large, yellowish stucco with red tile roofing. Employees were able to live in houses on the grounds, there was a playground for children, and employees with children shared childcare responsi-bilities. Families living on the grounds seemed to be a close knit and responsible group, rent was cheap, and utilities were included. There was a long waiting list for the houses.

From the outside, the state hospital was beautiful with pine trees and clean crisp air. The state hospital had many good benefits. South Dakota was very poor in the 1980's, second only to Mississippi. One of the most attractive benefits the state hospital provided to workers was Blue Cross medical insurance, essentially free health care for all who were employed. It was the only time in my entire life, until I turned 65, that I would ever have free health care.

The first floor included the kitchen dining area for staff and vis-itors, a large physical therapy and whirlpool room, and large offices for the administrative employees. Food for employees was served three times a day. It was unbelievably good. We ate food I had never tasted before, including halibut, shrimp, expensive cuts of beef served as roasts, and lasagna dishes. There were pies, cakes, fresh fruits, fresh salads, home baked bread and rolls, and all the milk, pop, coffee, and tea a person could drink. Everyone could eat for free, including our own family and friends, as well as the family and friends of residents. For me it was a wonderful place where I could go – even on my days off – and eat with my family, and the kids could play outside on the playground. The state hospital was a second home for many of us.

On the first day of work, we went on a tour of the hospital led by Joan, Director of Nursing. Two new employees were Sioux Indian women who were friends I knew from the past, one worked on the same cancer ward where I had worked. Most everyone in my group were very similar to me – women in their twenties and thirties with children and a husband who did not have a job. There were two men in our group, one was a kitchen help and one was a physical therapy aide.

We met in the cafeteria where she talked to us about the two floors where residents lived. Joan explained residents were usually called "kids" because they were not developed mentally, and many were as small as young children, but as old as an adult.

She explained, "Some of our kids here are in their late twenties and thirties. Few live to be much older. You will get used to them in time. Most are harmless and mean no harm; however, many are unable to control their actions. They are not mentally able to do ninety-five percent of what most of us do every day. Most are completely dependent on us."

We took the elevator to the first floor and stopped at the desk next to the elevator. It was the nurses' station where we met the nurse in charge. Next we started down the first hall and into the first room.

In the first bed was a young man of about twenty-five years old. He had a jumpsuit on and was making laughing and screeching sounds, moving back and forth in his bed, sitting up and laying down quickly, over and over. His bed resembled a large cage. It had a top, the sides were bars, and the door was made of bars. It appeared he could not get out at all. The bed was built with legs about three or four feet off the ground, and the crib was about three feet high, three feet wide, and five feet long. The front of the crib was exactly like the other sides with bars about two inches apart. The door was really the same as the front of the crib, except it had an iron clasp hidden on the bottom, which could only be reached from the outside. The aide would squeeze the metal clamp and hold the bars with the other hand, and while pushing up with the clamped hand, the door could be raised.

Joan moved away from the bed and said, "I do not want to open this door on Richard's crib because he moves very fast, so let's move over to Roger's and I'll try to show you what we do."

As we passed Richard's crib, he reached out toward us through the bars with his fingers and screamed and smiled a huge smile. I tried to remember by thinking, *this is Richard.*

After Richard and Roger, there were three more kids, all in the same type of beds. Some were sleeping or just lying there. A very small kid, Shane, was rocking back and forth and chewing on his hand. His hand was not bleeding, and I did not appear to be hurt, so I thought maybe he knew not to chew on it.

As we moved back out to the hall, Joan explained, "There are usually five kids in each room, and six rooms on each side of the hall. There are two different halls on the floor, separated by an activity room, where kids are brought to lay on mats or crawl around on the floor."

As we continued down the hall, two boys rolled near us. They wore helmets and hand mittens; one had knee pads on. One boy looked to be about fifteen, but he was about Richard's age – more like thirty. They rolled by us, making noises, and one would scream and appeared to be laughing a little.

I felt I could not work in this place and wanted to leave. I told a woman next to me I did not think I could work here. She agreed, saying she felt the same. The most difficult rooms were rooms where the kids really did look like little kids. They were young, maybe four to six years old. They had little socks and shoes, and tiny clothes, some were sitting up and strapped in little wheelchairs built just for them.

Our nurse explained, "Many of these people are likely blind, some blind and deaf. Some scream, perhaps as a way to reach out, maybe not because of pain or because they were trying to scare us. Many have seizures. All of you will follow a teacher aide for your first week. She will train you to lift, explain routines of bathing and meals, give you helpful hints while working with our kids, make sure you understand safety rules, and know the proper fitting of braces, clothing, and protective gear."

We continued our tour. Every room had four or five people, and most had a crib with a top. Some kids had stuffed animals pinned on their walls, because they could not hold them or play with them. The men and women were in separate rooms. There were small dressers with their names. There were no pictures or personal items on or in dressers – just room enough for one or two sets of clothes, if the kid could wear clothes. Many wore jumpsuits, which were tied up in back with heavy laces strung through strong eyelets.

Underneath each crib was a mat, which could be rolled out on the floor and used to lay on during the day and at mealtimes. Rooms were pretty noisy, and residents seemed to know we were visiting. Many would sit up and scoot toward us, or wring their hands and make noises which sounded like they were excited and interested in our group – like Richard, who we met first.

As we continued, we met several residents who were hydrocephalic, meaning they had a large head due to fluid in their heads. They were the kids who made me the saddest. They laid flat and had sandbag type pillows to hold their heads straight. Their heads were larger than their bodies, so if they needed to be moved, two aides would hold their head while another would hold their body. Their beds did not have covers and were more like regular cribs with high rails. As we approached, many kids were awake and able to look at us. One in particular, Shirley, seemed to smile at me. I cautiously waved at her a little.

As we walked away and back down the hall, we entered the clothing room and met Doris, who was in charge of clothes for the residents. There were clothing bins with small, medium, and large jumpsuits and different boxes with room numbers written above their box. There was a large box of cloth diapers, also. Nothing was folded because there were over one hundred kids on second floor. Doris showed us how to fold the diapers. They were large, cotton squares. She folded them into a kite and then added another in the middle, which was rectangular. There was also a large box with safety pins connected together on heavy strings, which we would use when pinning the diapers – they were knotted at each pin so they could not be removed. There were also shelves for a few sheets and blankets, because kids would tear them apart.

The room next to the laundry room was the breakroom. It was the place everybody smoked and drank coffee and talked. In the seventy's and eighty's, break rooms were always the same. Workers could smoke, drink coffee and pop, and eat food in the break rooms. When I worked on the cancer floor of the hospital, we all smoked in the breakroom. Smoke would roll in the air and down the halls in almost every nursing home and hospital I ever worked in during those years, just like Belden Manor.

Next was the activity room. Here kids rolled around on the floors, played with safe toys, and sometimes interacted. A small room was attached to the activity room but was separated by about a four foot wall. Aides and activity workers would be assigned for an hour or less during their shifts. Parallel to the activity room was the second hall with more rooms, including the shower room.

Finally, Joan paired us up with a training aide who would work with us for the next two weeks, and she left these encouraging words, "I try to pretend I am blind and deaf, sometimes, and it helps me understand the huge barriers many of our kids here are facing everyday of their lives. Also, it helps to remember they could be your own brothers and sisters."

We had wooden carts we pushed and used for linen, transporting kids, and transporting meal-trays. They were about the same height as the cribs and had about a two-inch ledge around the top, and a shelf underneath where we could keep clean clothes and supplies. We rolled them in and out of rooms. On bath mornings, which was almost every morning, we would lift our kids from their cribs and onto the cart, cover them with a bath blanket, and get in line to wait with other aides, who were also in line, to get a turn for the showers. There were four showers which were flat surfaces with a hose hanging from the ceiling. We lifted our kids onto the flat bath surface and sprayed them with the shower head and hose.

During the showers, some of the people in my group were very difficult and even combative. Probably because some aides were very careless and rough while they gave showers. They did not talk to the person, sometimes they failed to get the water at a good temperature, and often sprayed water directly into their faces. The very best therapy for residents were whirlpool sessions in the physical therapy room. Whirlpools were extremely comfortable and enjoyable to residents at the State Hospital.

No one in my group was able to eat sitting up. They had been taught to eat while lying on a mat in their room, and the aide would elevate their head on a head rest, sit next to them, and spoon feed them. Food was always pureed. It was either white potatoes or noodle, green veggies, tan meat, and a little gravy. The dessert was pudding. Meal Trays would come on the elevator stacked in a tall cart. We would take our trays, put them on our carts, and go from room to room with their trays. Meals took a long time, because we had to get everyone on their mats first, and then go back and feed them.

I used to say to Dolores, "Can we just say, 'I'm here to help you eat?' instead of yelling at our friends in the hall saying, 'Hey, I'm in room 4 with the feeders?'"

In the beginning, I thought people in my group were not able to think and did not know me. However, after talking to them for a few weeks, it appeared many kids were very aware of me and what was being said. One kid was Scotty. He was 32 years old, but he looked to be about eight years old, and if he could have a life free from the state hospital, he would be working with his father and doing chores on their farm. When he looked at me, he seemed kind of scared. Most everybody had chairs which were made especially for them by the physical therapy workers in the workshop on the grounds. The chairs were really perfect. Scotty's was small, he only weighed about fifty pounds, and it would lean back when he leaned back, so he had better control of his head. One day he was sitting in his chair, waiting for physical therapy to take him to the whirlpool downstairs.

"Scotty, Scotty, where are you going today?" I sang.

He turned his head and started laughing and kicking his feet. Then I quit singing and he looked afraid. I sang again, "Scotty, Scotty where is PT today, are they hiding somewhere outside and sleeping the time away?"

He started laughing, and the more I sang the more he laughed. Sometimes if he was in the hall, I would start singing. He would hear me coming and start laughing. I thought about "music being a universal language."

In the same room with Scotty was a person named Russell. Russell's body was shaped like an L. He was hard to dress and difficult to lift. He had a regular bed, and the head of the bed could be raised so he could watch a TV on the wall at the foot of his bed. When I started singing songs around Scotty, Russell looked annoyed. One day I started singing about a soap opera Russell was always watching, and I made fun of the actors and their drama. I pretended to cry and acted crazy like them.

Russell laughed.

Russell and I began to have better communication. He was non-verbal, like Scotty, but Russell was not retarded, in my view. He watched the news and followed stories. If an aide came in the room and tried to switch channels, Russell would get upset and try to yell at them. Later I learned Russell had Cerebral Palsy, and people with that disability are not retarded.

Working with "kids," like Russell and Scotty, made me think more about how everyone has a deep spirit inside themselves which is complicated and emotional. The saying "to thine own self be true" is a universal belief many people at the state hospital understood. Kids at the state hospital gave many of us new outlooks of gratitude and strength, and they taught us to be unapologetically true to ourselves.

Shirley was in my group, also. She was hydrocephalic. Three people needed to move her at all times – two would hold her head, and one would hold her body – in order to turn her in bed or lift her into her chair. Both Shirley and Russell had wide chairs, which were like a bed, and they barely fit through the door. Shirley was a very brave person. She had almost no hair, and her head drew a lot of attention. Shirley would get upset if she did not have her knitted hat on her head her mother made. One day a group of people from the Board of Charities and Correction toured our floor. There were well-dressed men and two very well-dressed, attractive women. When they came in Shirley's room, I was putting a quilt, that her mother had made, over her.

The group of people walked up and stood, looking at Shirley.

"This is Shirley, her mother made this quilt and knitted her hat as well," I said.

A well-dressed woman looked at Shirley and whispered, "That is the ugliest thing I have ever seen."

They turned and left with no more words. Shirley had a big tear coming down one of her eyes after they walked out of her room. She closed her eyes as if to tell me to go away. It was too much to see.

Richard was also in my group. I was afraid of Richard for about the first six months. He was very loud and always wanted to get out of his crib. Two people helped with him because he would grab on to your arms or hair and not let go. It was also hard to help Richard eat because he would try to grab the tray and put everything in his mouth at once. We would have to get him in his chair and secure his tabletop onto the chair so he could not get out. There was a chain on his chair we hooked onto the wall because he would wheel away if the brakes were off. I tried talking to Richard, I tried singing, and I tried explaining everything I was doing but nothing helped to get him to calm down a little.

"Richard, do you want to go for a walk down the hall?" I said one day.

He stared at me and became seriously quiet. So, I said, "If I take this railing down, will you just slow down and we can go for a walk?"

He seemed like maybe it was a "yes."

I slowly lowered the door and he put his legs over the edge, and I told him to hold on to me but not grab me. I believe we were both shocked this was actually happening. Very slowly he stood straighter. I was surprised how short and thin Richard really was. Slowly he took one step. He stood on his toes, then he took another step on his tiptoes. We made it to the door and started down the hall, passing the breakroom.

Someone from the breakroom yelled out, "Is that Richard Downey? Oh my god, that is Richard Downey!"

We walked carefully down the hall, turned around, and went back to his room. He got in his crib and I pulled the rail up. I was shocked and so was he. After that we walked every day, and soon PT was walking Richard. He was getting loud and began to walk much faster, but he walked down the hallways every day.

We had some good in-service meetings at the state hospital. One was a meeting where Joan tried to teach us empathy. She asked us to be the person who fed someone some soup and the other person would be fed. However, the person being fed had to wear a blindfold, and the person feeding could not talk to the person they were feeding. The "feeder" had to talk to everyone in the room, except the person she was "feeding." What happened was we could not tell when the soup was coming to our mouths, or where or what was even hitting our mouth.

Joan said, "That is how these people feel during mealtime. They do not know what is happening if you don't let them know." She did other exercises with us to help us understand how they might feel.

Working at the state hospital taught me how to understand some of the difficulties dependent people face, and it helped me appreciate my own health and my healthy kids. I owe so much to the residents at the state hospital. I know they are all gone now because many years have passed. I'm sure many people, like me, who care for the elderly and dependent, feel very privileged to be a guest in the lives of those who somehow believe in their own power, have taught us to be brave, and to not hesitate to break down walls. Working with people who were categorized as "severely and profoundly retarded" created a deep resentment inside of me. I feel it was a great injustice for anyone to be put into a box and labeled as somehow "less than" or "damaged."

There is a quote by the English poet John Milton (1608-74) from his poem *On His Blindness*.

He reflects that he, even with his disability, has a place in the world, saying, "They also serve who only stand and wait."

Maybe in the case of people who lived at the state hospital, it could be said, "they also serve who only sit and wait."

There are many wrongs residents of institutions endure. The most hurtful wrongs are those which treat people as "less than" and with indifference. As a nurses' aide, my focus began to change into thinking emotional care is more important than physical care on the scale of importance. I also embraced being a nurses' aide and no longer apologized for not being a nurse. My role in health care, for me, became more focused as a comfort caregiver, whose work was to understand what people needed in order to attain personal health and well-being, emotionally and physically. It taught me we all *do* have certain inalienable rights.

After five years at the state hospital, Don wanted to move to Seattle where his sister lived and there were more opportunities. I wanted to stay where we were, but we had 5 children to raise and we could not expect to have anything other than poverty if we stayed, so we left.

We were able to live in Don's sister's basement when we arrived in Seattle. We drove to her home with bald tires and no spare left, in a twelve-year old Mercury Comet and a car full of little kids. His sister moved to Seattle years earlier. Many young people from South Dakota would leave for better jobs – some would go to Minneapolis, others to Seattle.

The second day we arrived, I started working on the graveyard shift at a nursing home. Within a month, we found a very small, cheap house, which we rented. The house was structurally unsafe with leaks and mold. It was three miles from my job, and it was on a bus line. Don worked in construction and left at 5 A.M. Our kids were sometimes alone for almost two hours until I got home. I tried to work weekends and fewer weekdays, but we needed someone to be home in the early A.M. I hired a twelve-year old neighbor to stay with them until I got home. She tried hard to take care of everyone, but I worried constantly until I got home around 6:30 A.M.

# CHAPTER 6

## Nursing Homes and the Covid-19 Pandemic

During the mid-eighties, nursing homes in the state of Washington, and many other states, were no longer covered by a staff-to-patient law. The law required a nurses' aide could only care for a certain number of people per shift. Day shift aides could be assigned to no more than eight residents, swing-shift was twelve, and graveyard was twenty. I'm not sure of the exact ratio anymore, but if the mandate was not followed, the nursing home could be fined. We could call the state from any shift to report the staff shortage and someone from the state would make an unannounced visit.

Nursing homes, in many states, were required to follow the staff-to-patient ratio. It was a good law. However, lobbyists for nursing homes successfully lobbied to have the laws struck down. During this time, nursing homes became much worse, and as other states lost their battle to keep the staff-to-patient laws, nursing homes began making huge profits. Staff shortages were profitable for the big corporate chains. Nursing homes began to make more money per year than McDonalds and Burger King combined.

The removal of the staff-to-patient laws created huge holes in care, which were largely invisible to most people, but very profitable for the nursing home industry. When staff-to-patient laws were in effect, nursing home life was much more transparent. If a resident fell out of bed, or had bed sores, or was failing to thrive due to dehydration or lack of exercise, reasons for such misfortunes could be tracked to the amount of care residents received. However, this created negative results for nursing home audits and nursing homes began to lobby strongly against staff-to-patient laws.

The Covid-19 pandemic opened a curtain on nursing home care in America. For years residents, friends, and relatives have suffered under inadequate care in nursing homes. The most likely reasons for neglect and poor care is largely due to the giant nursing home chains who hire lobbyists to push for legislation which focuses on profits over people.

In an article by Judd Legum titled, *Legal Immunity from Grandma* May 27, 2020, he explains:

> "A recent report from the General Accountability Office (GAO) examined 'Infection prevention and control deficiencies in nursing homes in the years prior to the Covid-19 pandemic.' The GAO report found that between 2013 and 2017, 82% of the nation's 15,000 nursing homes had an infection prevention and control deficiency cited in one or more years. Almost 10,000 nursing homes were cited for multiple deficiencies over the time period."[6]

> He continues: "Across the country, at least 28,100 residents and workers have died from the coronavirus at nursing homes and long-term care facilities. The nursing home industry has spent more than $4 million on lobbying over the past year, employing more than a dozen full-time lobbyists."[7]

---

[6] Legum, Judd, "Legal Immunity From Grandma," *Popular.Info*.
[7] Ibid.

Finally, he concludes: "The problems at nursing homes have been exacerbated by a surge from private equity firms which have poured $5.3 billion into nursing home deals. Since 2015, overall private equity firms own 11% of nursing homes in the U.S." He cites a request by the nursing home industry in California, made to Governor Newsome, which "grants nursing homes broad immunity against residents who suffer injury or death during the pandemic."[8]

Nursing homes are regulated at the federal level by the U.S. Department of Health and Human Services, and at the state level by the State Department of Health and Human Services. The last federal legislation to regulate nursing homes was the Reform Act of 1987, more than thirty years ago. It established guidelines including residents' rights, behavior and assessments, nursing, dietary, and physicians. All nursing homes are required to comply with federal and state licensing requirements and to contract with Medicare and Medicaid services to be eligible to provide care.[9]

More than ten years later, in 2000, the National Citizens Coalition for Nursing Home Reform began to survey nursing homes across the country and reported "the greatest weakness in the 1987 Nursing Home Reform Act of 1987 was the failure to establish minimum staff-to-patient ratios."[10]

Table 3 of this study examines self-imposed regulations by some nursing homes in which "each resident received 84 minutes of total nurse and nurses' aide care during the 7 A.M. – 9 P.M. shifts, and only 3 minutes during the night shifts. Numerous studies regarding staff-to-patient discrepancies are more available since Covid-19 pandemic has created more questions about the nursing home industry in the U.S., as well as Canada." [11]

---

[8]  Ibid.
[9]  Ibid.
[10]  Ibid.
[11]  Ibid.

The for-profit nursing home chairs receive billions for care of our elderly and disabled. Medicaid payments are, at it's very least, $203 a day, and private care, at it's very least, is $247 a day. Those costs only cover the needs of the most healthy residents who are able to care for themselves and just need a home. However, any additional health concern adds more cost for care (Legum 2020).[12]

As nurses' aides, we are responsible for direct care. We do for the patient what the patient cannot do for themselves. Nurses' aides are trained and licensed to give direct care for residents who need assistance dressing, eating, walking, bathing, accessing bathrooms, getting in and out of beds, and general activities of daily living. The time we need is much more than we have, even as little as 45 minutes per day/per patient is not likely. This time would not include answering hall lights, helping with meals in dining rooms, transporting residents to activities, and bathing. This means the total number of residents assigned to a day shift aide should be no more than six residents, and that would leave the aide about 1¾ hour to do the "other" tasks, like answering lights, etc. So, under this schedule, it is unlikely residents will have timely care. Aides on day shift get people out of bed, into and out of bathrooms, dressed for breakfast, and into dining rooms to eat. After meals residents are taken back to bathrooms, beds are made, residents are helped into chairs, and are transported to activities. Residents who do not get out of bed are given breakfast in bed by whoever works as hall aides that day. After breakfast the assigned aide is responsible for getting those residents out of bed, or responsible for washing them in bed, dressing them, and making and positioning them in bed until the next meal. This is the common daily routine in nursing homes. All of these schedules do not include time aides spend relieving one another for breaks and meal breaks, and they do not include the shortage of aides when people call in sick.

Swing shift is a little less busy because there is only one meal and residents are usually through with transports. Night shift aides often

---

care for twenty or more residents, even though night shift is a very busy shift. There are few aides to answer light and bathroom trips, and many residents do not sleep well. Night shift aides also respond to high incidents of falls.

In truth most residents in nursing homes receive less than thirty minutes a day of direct care. If we were to consistently spend less than thirty minutes a day caring for every aspect of our lives or our children's lives, we would be neglecting many important issues. Critical care residents, such as patients with brain and spinal cord injuries, ALS and terminally ill patients, and patients who require ventilators to breathe do not have more time with nurses' aides than everyone else. In truth the residents who receive the most care and time are residents whose friends and families complain and file complaints.

Big corporate nursing home chains receive more money for residents who have the most physical needs. If gramma falls out of bed and breaks her hip, the nursing home receives more money for her than when she was able to walk. Nursing homes started putting feeding tubes into residents who were having issues eating or digesting food in the mid-eighties. Feeding tubes are extremely debilitating. Patients no longer go to the dining room to eat and no longer enjoy the social aspects of coffee and snacks.

I remember residents saying, "Oh that Thanksgiving meal smells so good." However, people who are fed through a feeding tube are more profitable to the nursing home industry.

Many relatives and friends feel guilt and betrayal when they cannot help the person they care for who is involved in nursing home life. They become worried and uncertain about what will happen if they complain. "Will my mother be treated worse if I complain?"

Most nursing homes provide semi-private rooms for residents, and a curtain separates the room. Often residents have little in common. An older woman in her eighties, who has hearing and vision loss, may have a roommate who is anxious and does not sleep well at night. This can be very stressful on an everyday basis for both residents, because they are unable to communicate. Often roommates are unhappy with one another because they are confused and misunderstand each other. More attention to placing residents in rooms where compatibility is considered is very important. How would we feel if we shared an apartment with someone we really did not get along with very well?

There are living conditions in nursing homes which are dangerous and wrong. Some residents remain in bed for days, weeks, and even months at a time. This happens because there is a shortage of nurses' aides in most nursing homes. Nurses' aides, and many nurses, call these people "bed patients" and "feeders." Management knows this is true but denies it exists. Bed patients have bed sores from being in bed. The bedsores seldom get better and usually become worse. Bed patients are fed meals in bed. They sometimes have tube feedings instead of meals. These are people who need the most care but get the least care. Many could be lifted out of beds and into chairs and be able to go to dining rooms for meals or sit outside in nice weather. The shortage of nurses' aides cause these bed patients to remain in beds because more than one aide is needed to get them up. Nurses' aides do not have time for that. If the aides spend thirty minutes getting a "bed patient" dressed, out of bed, and into the dining room, the other 10 people or more in their group are not being served and will not get to the dining room in time to eat.

The most vulnerable residents are "bed patients." They are most likely to die from pneumonia and infections and are the least able to defend themselves or verbally call for help. They are not always the oldest residents. Young people who are paralyzed or in comas due to accidents are likely to become "bed patients" unless they have family or friends to advocate for them on a regular basis. People with ALS are often "bed patients" who lie in bed every day, twenty-four hours a day. This is the untold reality of nursing home life. It has hardly changed since I started working in nursing homes more than fifty years ago. Profit over people creates injustices which are covered up by the people who make the profits.

There are many dangerous examples of care in nursing homes in America, which have not changed for a hundred years. A simple example no-one talks about is the bedpan. Bedpans are dangerous and cause skin tears and coccyx bedsores. Bed patients and patients who need help eating, are often dehydrated because there is not enough help to provide timely meals and fluids, and their skin becomes thin and frail. Often they are left on bedpans for long periods of time, again, "forgotten," and they have painful skin breakdowns. One of my homecare inventions is a bedpan which is made like a waterbed instead of the hard plastic or metal bedpans people have used for a hundred years or more.

Some management solutions, which would prevent the inadequate care of residents in long-term care facilities, would be:

Cameras in hallways, near time clocks, and in rooms requested by residents and/or families. Unless we have an accurate picture of how many aides are actually at work on any given shift, we cannot judge what the standard of care is for that shift. Nursing homeowners argue cameras violate privacy. Cameras are in daycare centers, schools, banks – nearly everywhere. Cameras should be in hallways of care centers to protect residents by recording how many people are working and how long residents are left in rooms, or sitting in hallways, during the day. If residents agree to have cameras in their rooms, they should be provided without cost.

Accountability for anyone acting as Power of Attorney. A second party mediator could intervene on behalf of family and residents.

Records for accountability need to be provided to friends and relatives, which allow them to make written requests for needs and wants of the resident. Responses concerning their requests need to be charted.

This type of charting is so important in nursing homes. Oftentimes relatives and friends express concerns or are informed of a resident's concerns, and there is no real place to make the report to an appropriate department. Concerns about drug and alcohol testing for staff should be documented, and random drug and alcohol testing of staff should be mandatory.

We all have a pretty good chance of coming into contact with nursing home life. When we first walk through the doors, we may not really notice something is wrong. However, as we travel through the hallways and into the heart of nursing home life, we will see it is dangerously broken. Beyond the front offices, lobbies, and rooms lies a world of chaos and indifference. This world does not exist because the people who work there don't care, it exists because nursing home big corporations rate profit before people. It is our responsibility to insist our state and federal legislatures bring back the staff-to-patient ratio laws which will open a door to accountability in nursing home care.

If I could design a care center for the elderly and disabled, I would create apartments to house two to four residents, and an aide would stay with them in that room for every shift. The apartments would be furnished, including comfortable recliners and hospital beds. They would have washers and dryers, a kitchen, whirlpool baths with lifts, complete access to internet and television. Meals could be made in the apartment or ordered in from the kitchen. There would be walk-in closets and clothes could be sent to the facility laundry or done in the apartment. Aides would be partnered with nurses and additional "helper aides" would be available at all times.

Residents who are diagnosed with dementia or Alzheimer's need to have things to do. In modern nursing homes, these residents pace the halls and are directed in and out of rooms, as if they were in a military barracks. My experience with people who have memory lapses, like Alzheimer's, are often willing and able to be active, and would like to do some of the same things they did in their past. Often many women and men enjoy shopping, arranging closets and hanging clothes, fixing appliances, working on food preparation – like peeling potatoes and apples – planting seeds, and raising indoor gardens. Nursing homes could arrange activity rooms where people could go "shopping" and have coffee or even eat in "cafes." My experience while caring for people with dementia, in my own home, helped me to create what I thought of as "safe centers," where "work" – like fixing items, folding clothes, creating scrap books, and filing papers – was part of the day.

There would be no big dining areas like the present-day nursing homes use. Elderly and disabled people in care centers today sit in huge dining rooms, waiting to eat with many people they do not know and become uncomfortable, cold, and tired. Residents who are placed in wheelchairs and pushed out of their rooms are "put" in the busy and crowded hallways, where they sit and wait for nothing. They are simply waiting. Some are waiting to be pushed back into their rooms, some are waiting to go to an activity, and some are just waiting because their room is being cleaned or their aide is too busy to take them back to their rooms.

Present day nursing homes have utility rooms where bedpans and urinals are spray- washed by hand and then left to dry. It is a duty for each aide to wash and clean the bedpans and urinals. The urinal and the bedpan have not been changed for more than hundred years. I have some time-tested designs for easier methods of self-care. One is a design for a better urinal, with balloon type attachments to a simple plastic neck. The entire urinal can be disposable or used long-term. It is spill-free and works great. I have tested it for years on people who lived in my own long-term care homes for the elderly and disabled. I have never applied for a patent because I do not have the funds, the same is true of my new and better bedpan. I would gladly give my ideas away to anyone who could seriously develop them.

Every care center should have comfortable family rooms and day-care for workers with children. Nursing homes in America are a huge money-making business. It's time for billionaires and charities to step up and redesign these care centers for all people who need long-term care. We will all experience a need for care at different times in our lives, and we are all responsible to give care to those people in our lives who are dependent and elderly.

One night when I was stressed out with my job and worried about my kids being alone for the morning hour, and I talked to my charge nurse and asked her,

"Do you have any ideas about what I should do? I make minimum wage, live in a house with a bad roof and mold on the walls, and my kids have a twelve-year-old neighbor girl babysitting at 5 A.M."

She suggested, "Maybe you should try taking care of people in your own home."

I answered, "But my house is a one bedroom with not enough space for my own family."

She explained to me, "You could get an adult family home license if you attend a weekend class at the Red Cross building for one weekend." She added, "maybe if you get a license for a home, you could get a home."

I attended the class within the month and did get a license. The number of people I could take care of would depend on the state licensor inspecting my house. Now I needed a house and a miracle.

Looking through the paper, I found an ad for a house. I still remember the ad.

*Four bedroom Tudor house with panoramic view.*

The house was not far away and in a busier side of town. I called the number and made an appointment to meet the owner, Steve Rosenthal. Don was not very interested, so I went by myself and brought the kids.

The house was beautiful, I thought. It had an apple tree and a back yard, two bedrooms upstairs, and two larger bedrooms downstairs. I never imagined living in a nicer home. We lived in a small, rundown trailer in South Dakota, and, in all my life, I never expected to be looking at this type of house.

Mr. Rosenthal was an older man who seemed really attentive to my questions.

I asked, "How much do you need for me to move in here? I am trying to start a home for my family, and for the elderly and disabled. I just got a license from the state."

He said, "The rent is seven-hundred and fifty dollars a month. First and last, and a seven-hundred dollar deposit."

"I really need and want this house. I can't pay you much right now, but I can give you forty dollars. I'll pay the first month and part of the deposit next month and make rent and pay off the deposit and last month as the time goes. I will sign a deal," I said.

Fortunately he was very kind and seemed to be somewhat of a risk-taker, and he definitely looked like he thought I was saying something confusing.

His deal went like this, "I will drop the last month, but leave the deposit and give you the first two months free. Deal?"

How could I not be shocked and grateful?

We lived in this house for about four years. My kids went to school at the Catholic school across the street. It was the best for us because I rarely had a car and could always run across the street and get one of the kids if they got sick or had problems. The church was a great community for me. I am not a religious person, but I do believe there is a Spirit in the universe. However, the Catholic Church was a great help to me and my family. They had a shelter next to the church for women and children. Sometimes kids from the shelter would come to our house and play in the backyard with my kids in the summer and after school. The nun would visit us, and so would the priest, sometimes.

The first year we lived in this house, Don did not want to stay anymore, and I lost my license. I was taking care of four people at the time, along with our five kids. I believe it was too stressful for Don. I am an extreme caregiver and probably difficult to live with twenty-four hours a day. Before Don left, he met someone else and seemed much happier. I filed for a divorce, in which he agreed to pay only twenty-five dollars a month for each of our kids, and he agreed they could stay with me if he could take them out a couple of times a week to eat pizza and visit his sister. So that was the deal. Except, before we got divorced, the lawyer found we were never married. We thought we got married years ago, but the judge never filed it.

I only took in two people, because a person could care for two people without a license. I would have to apply for a license again, since Don left, so I began working graveyard in nursing homes. A young woman from the shelter agreed to help me at nights by staying with my kids and the residents if she could live in a small room off the kitchen. After about three years, we moved to a larger house, where I applied for a license for three people and we continued for nearly ten more years, until my kids were in high school or graduated.

# CHAPTER 7

We took care of people in our home for over twelve years. All of my kids helped me so much in those years. I hardly left the house and would sometimes hire a neighbor to get groceries, but when my kids got older, they got groceries for me.

During these years, I discovered many ways to care for the elderly and disabled which were different from what I had learned in the hospitals and nursing homes where I worked. First I charged people what they could afford, instead of a rate according to what was wrong with them. Most people who lived with us were retired, working people who had small pensions or social security. Nursing homes make most of their money from Medicaid, which they can hike up by having patients with many different problems, at least on paper. However, family homes could not get Medicare payments or Medicaid, and that was the difference. This law kept family homes out of the loop for any significant payments. Nursing homes were getting up to seven thousand dollars from Medicaid for the same person who could only pay me privately, out of their pension, about seven hundred dollars. Also, nursing homes would take the patient's pension and property.

I took care of longshoremen, bus drivers, postal workers, government workers, and private families who wanted to keep their relatives out of nursing homes. Sometimes I took care of clients who had tried to save up for retirement but had health issues. I always kept it fair, and people who lived with us were able to feel like they were not being ripped off. My kids worked in fast food, paper routes, and other places as they grew up, so they bought most of their clothes and other stuff they wanted.

During those years, we cared for nineteen people. One woman lived with us for nine years, some others for around five years, and others between one and four years. Many people were over eighty years old when they came; some were in their nineties. Most had either lived on their own or were cared for by family members. In a way, it was good I was not a nurse, because I was able to call nurses for help at any time. They would make house calls and do visits and home care, if needed. No one who lived with us suffered any falls, skin breakdowns, or accidental injuries.

If more people could understand the need for family homes for the elderly and disabled, everyone involved in this care method could appreciate its benefits. If a parent could be paid from $2,000 to $4,000 to care for a person in their home, they could stay home and save money on childcare and transportation to and from work and outside their home.

Our elderly and disabled family and friends are a great natural resource for all of us. Unfortunately, the nursing home industry has claimed many people for their own financial gains.

I tried to imagine what kind of room a person would have in their own home. I needed to understand the person who I was caring for and to communicate with each person about what they wanted and needed in their own opinion, not mine. I needed to know what gave them comfort and what they needed to feel good about their place in my home.

We probably could all agree our rooms are our comfort zones. But as people age and begin to need adaptive measures for their everyday lives, we need to try to understand their physical and emotional comfort zones. Elderly and disabled people need to feel safe and understood. Communication is the first step toward understanding our common wants and needs.

One of the first people to live with us was a longshoreman who was born in Yugoslavia in 1894, and whose family immigrated to America and worked in coal mines. He had been kicked out of nursing homes for being belligerent to the help. A discharge planning office from a hospital called and asked if I had a room for him. He could pay seven hundred dollars a month for rent. We met at the hospital and agreed to try working together. This would be my first real test to create a comfort care room. His name was Bill.

When Bill arrived, he was barely able to walk and had a cane. Exhausted as he came through the door, he sat at the kitchen table and laid his head down on his crossed arms. I was nervous about him seeing all of my kids, because they were still very young and could be quite noisy and busy.

I sat next to him and said, "I have five children; oldest is eight, youngest is three now. Do you like children?'

Bill answered, "I have never been married or had children, but they are ok. I love confusion." He continued with, "Where is my room? I need to lay down."

He was over six feet tall, and I tried to help him stand up from the table, but he pushed his cane against my leg and said.

"I need to get up on my own, and if I fall you need to watch out."

This was my first clue. Bill was very independent and also very kind, because he was more concerned that he may fall on me than the fact he may fall.

He slept for nearly twenty-four hours straight the first day, to the point I was afraid he may die. I later understood Bill would often stay awake for an entire twenty-four hours, and then sleep for the next twenty-four. It was his pattern.

He would explain, "Working as a longshoreman, we would work for days at a time before we slept."

Bill loved sitting in our living room, watching the kids play, and would laugh when they wrestled and fought.

He'd say, "That littlest one of yours will take them all down at once when they all get bigger."

Talking about his experience at the nursing home, he would swear a lot.

"Them people would not give me a cigarette or a glass of whiskey, and they stole my wool socks. That's all I wanted and they didn't care, damn bastards."

Part of Bill's care then, for him, was sitting in the recliner on his good days. After the kids were in bed, he would have a couple of cigarettes and a bit of whiskey.

"This is my only pleasure I have left in life," he would say.

There were recliners for everyone in our home. Many older people do really well with recliners next to their beds. Nighttime is sometimes difficult when people get older, there are trips to the bathroom, aches and pains, and sometimes just no appetite for sleeping. A recliner is a safe place for those times. In nursing homes, people have a high rate of falls at night, likely due to getting in and out of bed.

Mealtime in nursing homes is an uneasy time for residents. In the morning, many elderly people who lived with us liked to sit in their recliners instead of the table, because the elderly often need time to "warm up" and time to wake up. I would make warm drinks and warm cereals, like oatmeal, and use light weight plastic cups with large handles for them in the morning. Elderly people, in general, eat small meals throughout the day. Nursing homes create a mealtime designed for a busier and work-oriented life.

The elderly have a style unique to them. Nice clothing without zippers and buttons is important in their world. They enjoy easy access to windows and music, plants and animals, and visits with children and families.

In 1997 my kids were growing up and starting to leave. My oldest son joined the Navy and everyone else had jobs. My sister, Nancy, committed suicide in the Heaven's Gate Mass Suicide Cult in San Diego, California. It was March of 1997. I turned on the afternoon news on CNN and saw the story. Next to my TV was a cedar chest my father had made for Nancy, which she left with me a few years earlier when she told me she was giving all her possessions away and joining "Total Overcomers Anonymous." That was the name of the cult before it became, "Heaven's Gate."

We talked for days before she left. She showed me tapes of "Doe" talking. I tried to talk her out of leaving, and that she could be joining a cult, but she would not listen. Still, when I saw the news, I was shocked. They had a 1-800 number to call, and I found out Nancy was one of the people who died in the cult suicide. I called home and my mother answered. I asked to talk to my father, but she said he died a few months earlier on November 11th – Veterans Day.

"Why didn't you call me?" I asked. She was silent and did not answer.

"Nancy died in the mass suicide in California, today," I said, crying.

She hung up. The next day, my brother Tom called and told me they were going to have Nancy's body returned home and they would bury her there. There was nothing I could say. I was in Seattle. I had not been home in years due to not having enough money, and I had no one who could help with my children and residents in my home for such an extended trip. No one ever called me after Nancy's suicide. The phone was silent.

I did not go to Nancy's funeral and had not been contacted when my father died only two months prior. I just cried, every day. I quit my business because I could not do much. I cried when I was doing dishes, trying to get meals, and helping people get dressed. Within that week, I called my licensor and said I had to quit and did not want my license anymore. I needed someone to help me find a better place for the two people who were still living with us because I could not do it anymore.

After about a month, I moved to a small apartment with my two youngest kids, who were still living at home. I went to a mental health facility to apply for a job.

Sitting in the personnel office and talking to the Director of

Nursing, I said. "My sister killed herself in the Heaven's Gate cult and I cannot stop crying. I need to either just live here or work here."

She said, "How about trying to work here? I'll put you on next month's schedule."

I began working again in June 1997. Within a few months, a resident from the facility, who was unable to walk and had MS, asked if he could move in with me and my last two children who were still at home. He was in a wheelchair, and unable to get out of bed on his own or move around much. I believed he would only get worse in the mental health facility, and MS was not a mental disorder. He lived with us for over twelve years.

By 2017 I had been caring for grandchildren and working as a nurses' aide, but I wanted to go to Aalborg, Sweden and visit a nursing home known as "The Best Nursing Home in the World." The office at the Aalborg Nursing Home said I could visit anytime and give them some of my inventions for care in nursing homes.

# CHAPTER 8

A couple of years earlier, I met an eccentric sort of hermit through Ancestry who lived in Sweden. He traveled and spent many younger years as a vagabond, and in Copenhagen as a baker. I called him and asked if he would go with me to Aalborg to visit the nursing home and if he could help me get there and translate for me. He said he would go with me if I met him at his place, which was in a small village in Sweden. My son bought me a round trip plane ticket, good for five days, and I flew to Copenhagen and took the train to the town outside of his village and a taxi to his hut.

His name was Bjorn and he was 75 years old. We had spent hours e-mailing and talking online for over three years. He said he was a piano player and had an old Steinway Grand Piano in his hut. He loved his piano and would often tell his story about how he had removed a side wall of his hut many years earlier to get his Steinway inside, then boarded up the wall, so no one could steal his piano. Bjorn was a social activist, suspicious of America, but a strong supporter of Bernie Sanders (who I was supporting). He had thick, unruly hair, was very thin, but fairly average in most every other way, except for his eyes, which moved quickly and curiously.

Bjorn did not have visitors and lived a solitary life. He did have a cell phone but no electricity and only a pump outside for water. He began showing me through his house as soon as I entered. The hut was small. In the narrow entry was his table for meals and coffee. After a few feet, and a left turn, was his living room with his Steinway, a wall of books on one side, and a huge wood stove on the other side. There was a sofa between the two walls and a rocking chair in front of the wood stove. On the other side of the entry were two small bedrooms and a small kitchen/washroom at the end of the hall. We walked back to the living room, where he motioned for me to sit down on the couch as he put wood into his stove. It was getting dark, so he lit some candles and the fireplace also lit the room.

On the woodstove was a coffee pot. "Do you want coffee?" He asked as he began pouring it into cups. Before I could answer, he gave me a large cup of coffee, sat down in front of his stove and said, "When did you leave Copenhagen?"

I answered, "It took me about three hours to get here, so three hours ago. I took the train and people were really nice. I couldn't figure out what train to get on from the airport and I thought no one could speak English, but nearly everyone did. A woman showed me where to wait and another woman even stayed with me until I got on the train. She told people on the train where I was going and to tell me when to get off."

Bjorn laughed. Then he said, "I did not think you would really come here to Sweden. I am surprised."

He continued. "I do not have visitors here often. Only my cousin, Karla. She comes here about twice a year. We do not get along, but she is a visitor and family. Are you hungry?"

I was, but I said, "No, I'm not at all hungry. Do you have a bathroom?"

He stood up and said, "Follow me."

We walked down the short hall to the washroom/kitchen. There was a washbowl and a small table next to a commode. "This is for girls, I tell Karla. I use the one outside when you are here."

When I returned to the living room, Bjorn wanted to play his Steinway for me. It was not in very good shape, missing Ivories, some keys would stick, and it needed to be tuned.

Bjorn was a good piano player, however. "I play mostly classical," he said.

I was really tired and asked, "Where can I sleep, and can we talk more tomorrow? I just have to lay down."

"Yes, of course let me show you."

He showed me one of the small rooms saying, "This is where Karla sleeps when she visits. You will notice the books, eyeglasses, and slippers are hers." He took some blankets out of a small closet at the end of the bed, "These are all clean, she always washes everything when she leaves. Look at this blanket, you don't wash it because it is a feather blanket. Have you ever had one?"

"No, I have never even seen one. Thank you so much," I said.

As he turned to leave, he said, "Look, this is my room."

I looked in the door and it was a very small bunk bed with more feather blankets. We said goodnight, and after I laid down and covered up with my feather blanket, I heard the Steinway piano playing, again, classical music.

The next day, I realized Bjorn had very little food and seemed quite poor. He was also not in good health. I heard him coughing throughout the night and he did not sleep well. I could hear the door to his hut open and close many times throughout the night. It didn't bother me, because I took care of people in my homes for many years, but I knew he was not doing well when I saw him again that morning. He was sitting on his couch with his head back and sleeping. When he awoke, he was confused.

"Well, when did you get here. How was Copenhagen?" he asked.

I answered as if his questions were perfectly reasonable and changed the subject. "Do you have any coffee?"

He walked to the back "kitchen" and returned, saying, "I meant to tell you, I'm waiting for Karla to bring me some groceries."

He sat down at his stove and began building a fire. Soon he was asleep again in his rocking chair. I went outside and noticed a house not too far away where a young man was standing, smoking. He waved to me and we walked toward one another. He spoke English, was about twenty-five years old, and said he had lived in Los Angeles for a time, but this was his home and he had known Bjorn for years.

"Bjorn told me he was expecting a visitor. I thought it was Karla, but she doesn't come here, only every six months, and she just left a few weeks ago. She is his cousin and she tries to check on him, I take him groceries when I can. He can't afford much."

I explained to him who I was, and I was going to Aalborg on the train with Bjorn to see the "World's Best Nursing Home" in Aalborg, Denmark.

"Sorry," he said. "But I'm afraid Bjorn is in no shape for a trip like that. I don't know what to do with him. He is getting old, harvests the magic mushrooms here in the woods, gets high, and is losing his focus. I cannot afford to buy food for him and my own family, and Karla is of little help."

I thanked him for explaining Bjorn to me and went back to the hut. The following days, I worked around Bjorn's hut, cleaning, washing dishes and clothes, cutting and carrying branches and wood inside. I felt Bjorn knew me but confused me with Karla.

When his neighbor came to visit Bjorn that day, I asked him, "What do you do when Bjorn needs food?'

He said, "I get him coffee, canned goods, pasta and cakes, if I can afford it. Karla leaves a small amount for me to stretch throughout the months until she returns"

I had changed about one hundred and twenty dollars into "Kroner, Denmark's National Bank" at the airport, and gave his neighbor, Hans, all of it, except enough for me to get some water before I got back on the plane in Copenhagen. I decided to go to Aalborg another time and to spend another few days with my friend.

Hans brought a lot of good food back for Bjorn and we all arranged a place in his bedroom for canned goods, coffee, beans, rice, cookies, and some bread and jelly. The day I needed to leave, Hans brought me to the train, which went from Sweden back to Copenhagen. Before I left, Bjorn seemed angry, but gave me a huge hug and said, "You know you cannot leave, it's a 30-day minimum stay here."

But we both knew I could not stay. I continued sending Hans money for Bjorn for nearly a year, until Bjorn no longer corresponded with me and Hans told me he was placed in a facility for his own care in Stockholm. I always thought we would meet up again. The day before I left, we were both walking down a dirt road and he said, "We are, really, just two old people."

Of course I disagreed, but he was being truthful.

Aalborg Nursing Home in Aalborg, Sweden is a place I wish we could create for the elderly and disabled in America. A place where two to three people could share a room, equipped with cooking and laundry. Nurses' aides would be assigned to take care of only those people. There would be daily visits from dietary aides for help with food preparation and visits from bath aides for bathing would be included, if needed.

Within the facility, like in Aalborg, would be coffee houses, shopping, and cafes designed specifically for the elderly and disabled. The shopping area would also be available to outside visitors, but they would be required to have passes. Pets would be allowed, and there would be a pet activity and play center, including a pet shop. There would also be a daycare for children and a game room for older children who come to visit with their parents.

We can change the design of life for the elderly and dependent if we recognize the stigma which has created our nursing homes in America. We have to create a more caring and healthy environment for our families and friends who have been in our lives for many years. The space between the young and the old needs to be filled in with new and positive change in long-term care.

Relentless struggles for peace and justice by Black Lives Matter, climate change activists, progressive politics, and many younger people who are actively seeking real change are tearing down injustices of "man's inhumanity to man."

Helen Keller, who became blind and deaf at a very young age believed we should never accept indifference and negativity, writing, "While all the world is full of suffering, it is also full of overcoming."

# BIBLIOGRAPHY

Legum, Judd. "Legal Immunity From Grandma." *Popular Info.*
   *https*://popular.info/p/legal-immunity-from-grandma

Torrey, E. Fuller. "Ronald Reagan's Shameful Legacy: Violence,
   The Homeless, Mental Illness." *Salon.* September 29, 2013.

https://www.salon.com/2013/09/29/ronald_reagans_shameful_le
   gacy_violence_the_homeless_mental_illness/.